NORTH AMERICAN ANIMALS

Blue Jays

by Betsy Rathburn

BELLWETHER MEDIA • MINNEAPOLIS, MN

Note to Librarians, Teachers, and Parents:

Blastoff! Readers are carefully developed by literacy experts and combine standards-based content with developmentally appropriate text.

Level 1 provides the most support through repetition of high-frequency words, light text, predictable sentence patterns, and strong visual support.

Level 2 offers early readers a bit more challenge through varied simple sentences, increased text load, and less repetition of high-frequency words.

Level 3 advances early-fluent readers toward fluency through increased text and concept load, less reliance on visuals, longer sentences, and more literary language.

Level 4 builds reading stamina by providing more text per page, increased use of punctuation, greater variation in sentence patterns, and increasingly challenging vocabulary.

Level 5 encourages children to move from "learning to read" to "reading to learn" by providing even more text, varied writing styles, and less familiar topics.

Whichever book is right for your reader, Blastoff! Readers are the perfect books to build confidence and encourage a love of reading that will last a lifetime!

This edition first published in 2018 by Bellwether Media, Inc.

No part of this publication may be reproduced in whole or in part without written permission of the publisher. For information regarding permission, write to Bellwether Media, Inc., Attention: Permissions Department, 5357 Penn Avenue South, Minneapolis, MN 55419.

Library of Congress Cataloging-in-Publication Data

Names: Rathburn, Betsy, author.
Title: Blue Jays / by Betsy Rathburn.
Other titles: Blastoff! Readers. 3, North American Animals.
Description: Minneapolis, MN : Bellwether Media, Inc., [2018] | Series: Blastoff! Readers. North American Animals | Audience: Ages 5-8. | Audience: K to Grade 3. | Includes bibliographical references and index.
Identifiers: LCCN 2017028795 | ISBN 9781626177284 (hardcover : alk. paper) | ISBN 9781681034690 (ebook)
Subjects: LCSH: Blue jay–Juvenile literature.
Classification: LCC QL696.P2367 R38 2018 | DDC 598.8/64–dc23
LC record available at https://lccn.loc.gov/20170287956

Editor: Rebecca Sabelko   Designer: Josh Brink

Printed in the United States of America, North Mankato, MN.

Table of Contents

What Are Blue Jays?

Blue jays are colorful birds that fly across much of North America.

blue jay range = ☐

conservation status: least concern

Extinct
Extinct in the Wild
Critically Endangered
Endangered
Vulnerable
Near Threatened
Least Concern

These songbirds are found throughout the eastern half of the United States. They live as far north as southern Canada.

Blue jays live in many **habitats**. They are found in backyards, parks, and forests.

Some blue jays **migrate** in the winter. They fly south in search of warm weather.

Blue Beauties

Blue jays are bright blue birds. White and black bands line their wing feathers. Their bellies are gray or white.

Identify a Blue Jay

blue feathers

black bill

crest feathers

Crest feathers on their heads rise when the birds are surprised or angry.

Blue jays have long, rounded
tails. They have dark eyes
and black bills.

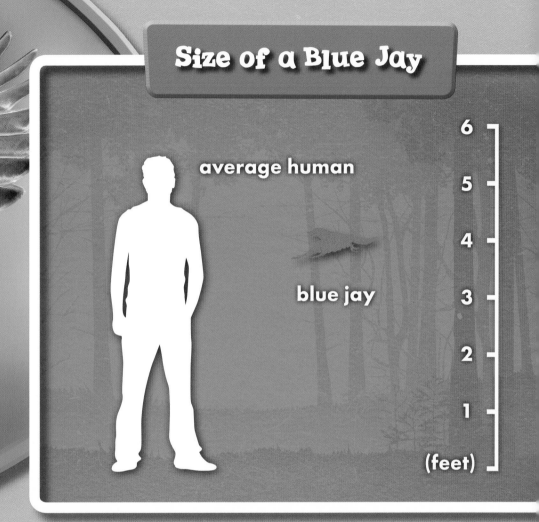

The largest blue jays grow to be
12 inches (30 centimeters) tall. A
17-inch (43-centimeter) **wingspan**
is common for many blue jays.

Blue jays are known for their loud calls. These birds can even **mimic** other bird sounds! The jays use calls to **communicate** with one another.

raccoons

gray squirrels

house cats

screech owls

American crows

Virginia opossums

They warn other blue jays of nearby **predators** such as squirrels and raccoons.

13

These **omnivores** mostly eat nuts, fruits, and seeds. Sometimes, they eat insects and small animals.

On the Menu

acorns

DeKay's snakes

beechnuts

sunflower seeds

American
grasshoppers

red-backed
salamanders

Blue jays often carry food in
their throat pouches. Then, they
hide it for later. These birds do
not mind leftovers!

Each year, male and female blue jays gather sticks, moss, and leaves. Then, they work together to build a nest.

When their work is done,
females lay up to seven eggs.

Females sit on their eggs to keep them warm. In about 18 days, baby blue jays **hatch**. Mom and dad take turns bringing food to their hungry **chicks**.

Name for babies:	chicks
Number of eggs laid:	2 to 7 eggs
Time spent inside egg:	17 to 18 days
Time spent with parents:	up to 2 months

Soon, the young birds get their flight feathers. These **fledglings** explore the branches near their nests.

After a month or two, the fledglings are ready to leave for good. Fly away, blue jays!

Glossary

chicks—baby blue jays

communicate—to share information and feelings

crest—a bunch of feathers on top of a blue jay's head

fledglings—young birds that have feathers for flight

habitats—lands with certain types of plants, animals, and weather

hatch—to break out of an egg

migrate—to travel from one place to another, often with the seasons

mimic—to copy closely

omnivores—animals that eat both plants and animals

predators—animals that hunt other animals for food

wingspan—the distance between the tip of one wing to the tip of the other

To Learn More

AT THE LIBRARY

Alderfer, Jonathan. *National Geographic Kids Bird Guide of North America: The Best Birding Book for Kids from National Geographic's Bird Experts.* Washington, D.C.: National Geographic, 2013.

Mara, Wil. *Blue Jays.* New York, N.Y.: Cavendish Square Publishing, 2015.

Ponka, Katherine. *A Bird Watcher's Guide to Blue Jays.* New York, N.Y.: Gareth Stevens Publishing, 2016.

ON THE WEB

Learning more about blue jays is as easy as 1, 2, 3.

1. Go to www.factsurfer.com.

2. Enter "blue jays" into the search box.

3. Click the "Surf" button and you will see a list of related web sites.

With factsurfer.com, finding more information is just a click away.

Index

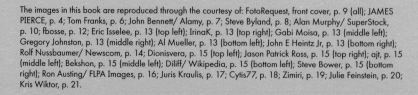